MW00938229
THIS
BOOK
BELONGS
TO

ARDAAS

Sat Sri Akaal!

Welcome, dear young readers, to the enchanting world of "Ardaas: Little Hands, Big Prayers." In this magical journey, we explore the heartwarming prayer, "Ardaas Tum Thakur." It's a special conversation with the universe, filled with wishes, thanks, and love. Ardaas is a superpower that connects us to something greater than ourselves—a way of expressing gratitude for the good things, seeking help when needed, and spreading love to everyone around us. It's our secret code to contribute to making the world a better, happier place.

As we turn the pages, you'll not only learn the words in both English and Punjabi but also discover their profound meanings. The vibrant pictures serve as a fun guide, illustrating why Ardaas is special and how it can fill your heart with warmth and positive vibes.

Let's begin by praising the glory of Waheguru Ji, acknowledging the divine power, and seeking blessings and guidance at the feet of the Almighty. Our prayers extend for the protection and well-being of our families.

We echo heartfelt requests for a kind and grace-filled life, brimming with the blessings of Waheguru Ji.
Remember, "Ardaas Tum Thakur" is like a heart-to-heart talk with Waheguru Ji, where we express love, gratitude, and seek guidance for a happy and blessed life. It's a ritual of respect to cover the head, fold hands, and stand while performing the Ardaas, bowing down upon its completion.

May this journey through "Ardaas: Little Hands, Big Prayers" inspire you to embrace the beauty of this ritual and fill your hearts with the warmth of love and gratitude.

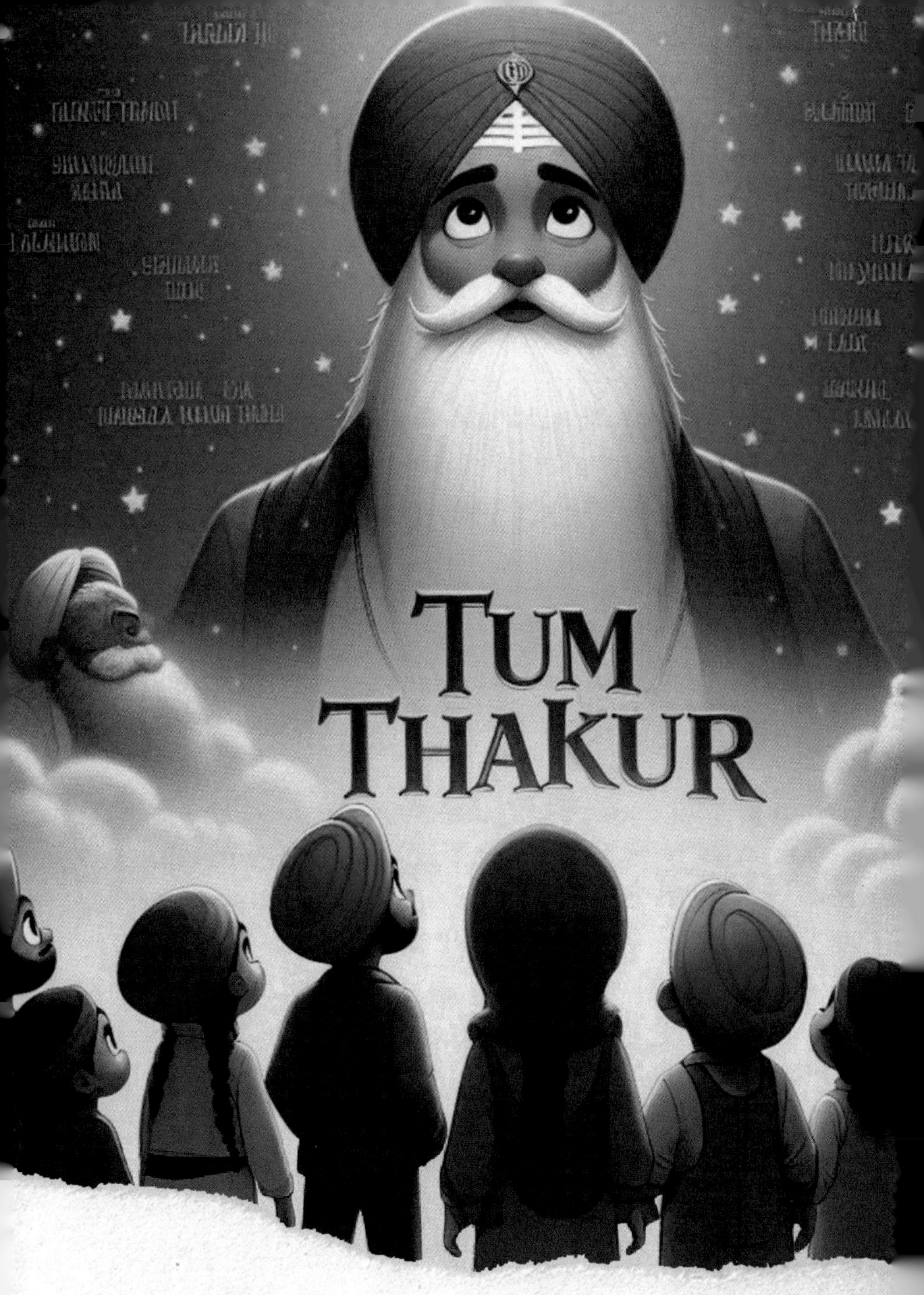

ਤੂ ਠਾਕੁਰ

YOU ARE OUR MASTER

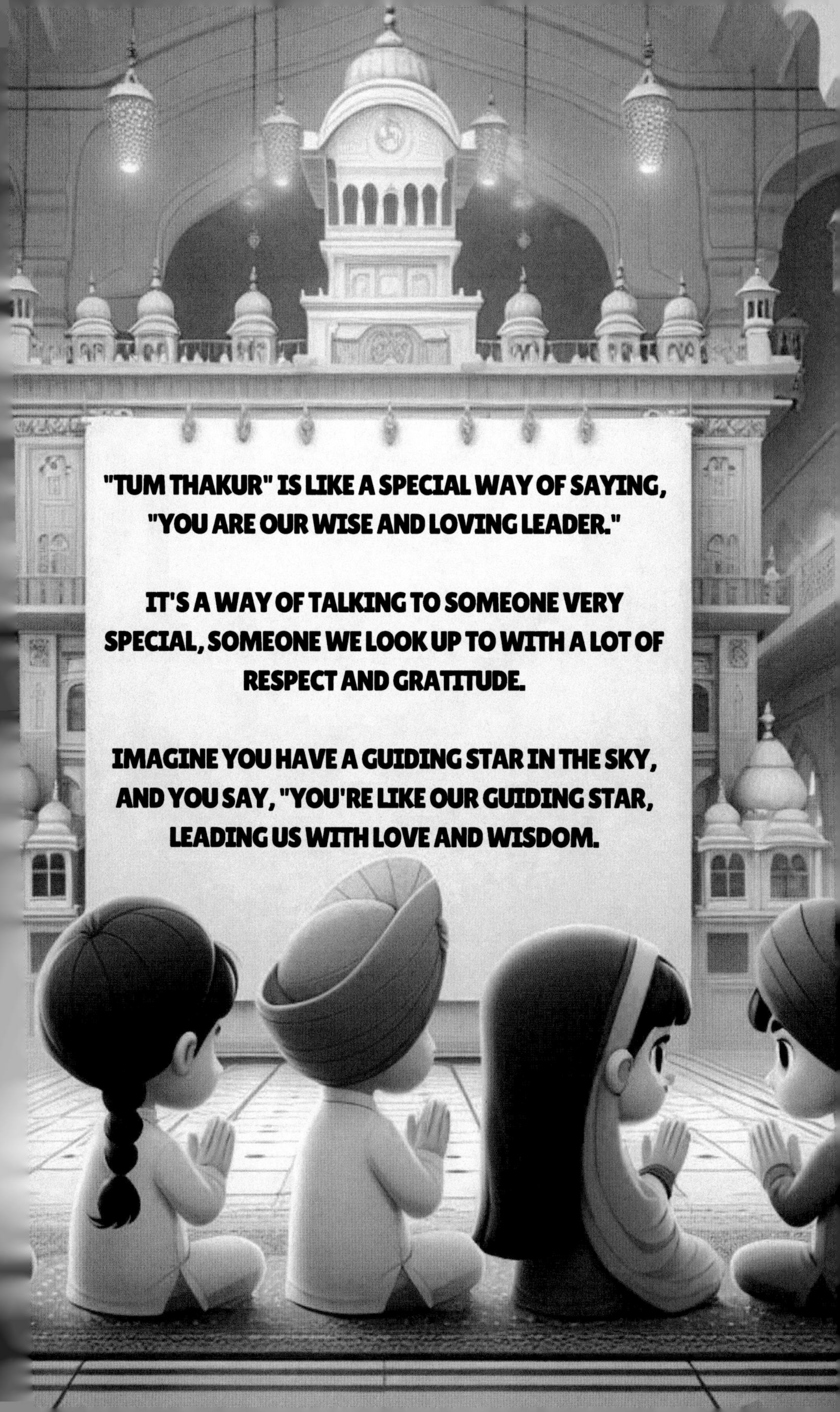

"TUM THAKUR" IS LIKE A SPECIAL WAY OF SAYING, "YOU ARE OUR WISE AND LOVING LEADER."

IT'S A WAY OF TALKING TO SOMEONE VERY SPECIAL, SOMEONE WE LOOK UP TO WITH A LOT OF RESPECT AND GRATITUDE.

IMAGINE YOU HAVE A GUIDING STAR IN THE SKY, AND YOU SAY, "YOU'RE LIKE OUR GUIDING STAR, LEADING US WITH LOVE AND WISDOM.

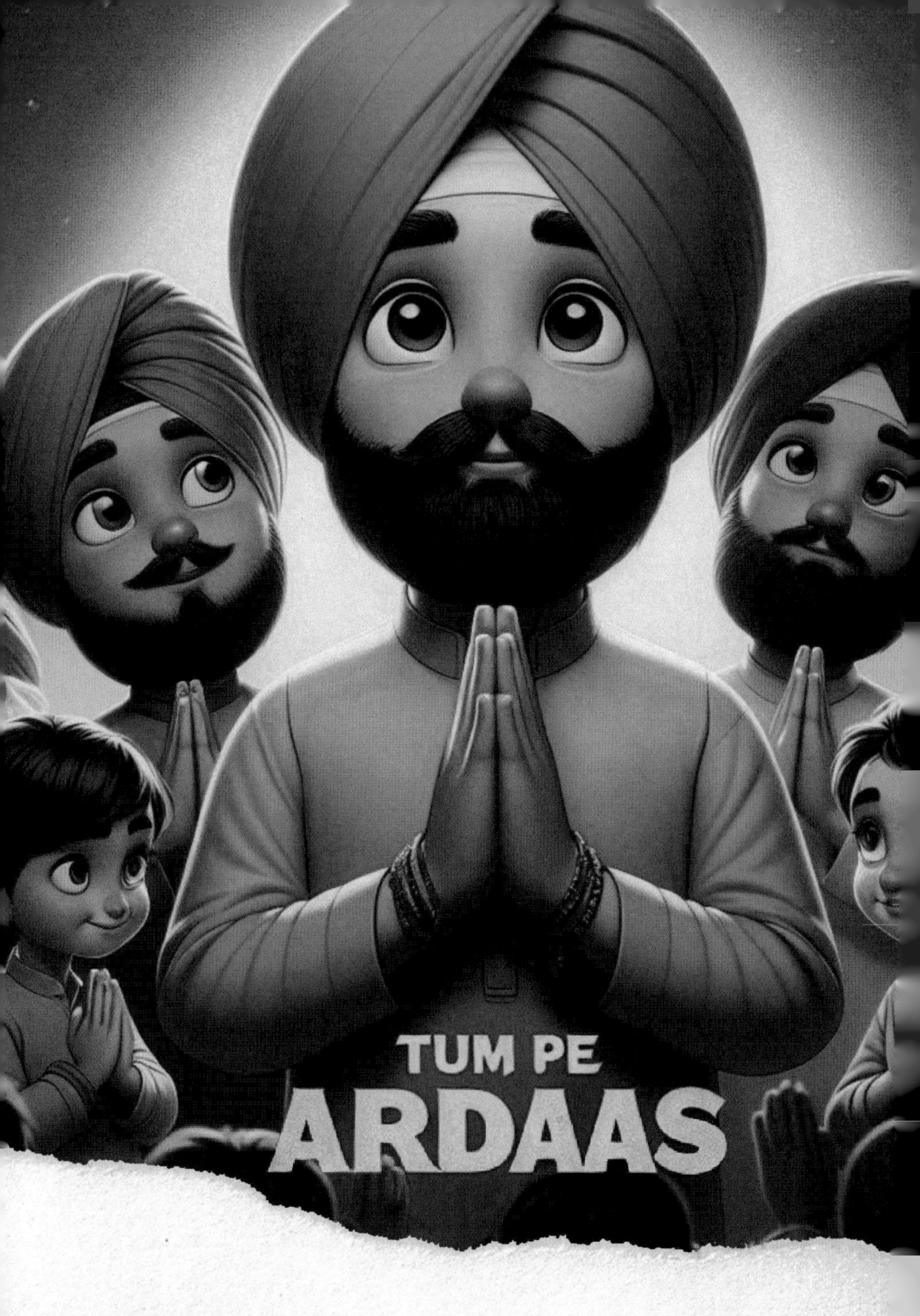

ਸਤਿ ਨਾਮੁ

TO YOU, I OFFER THIS HUMBLE PRAYE

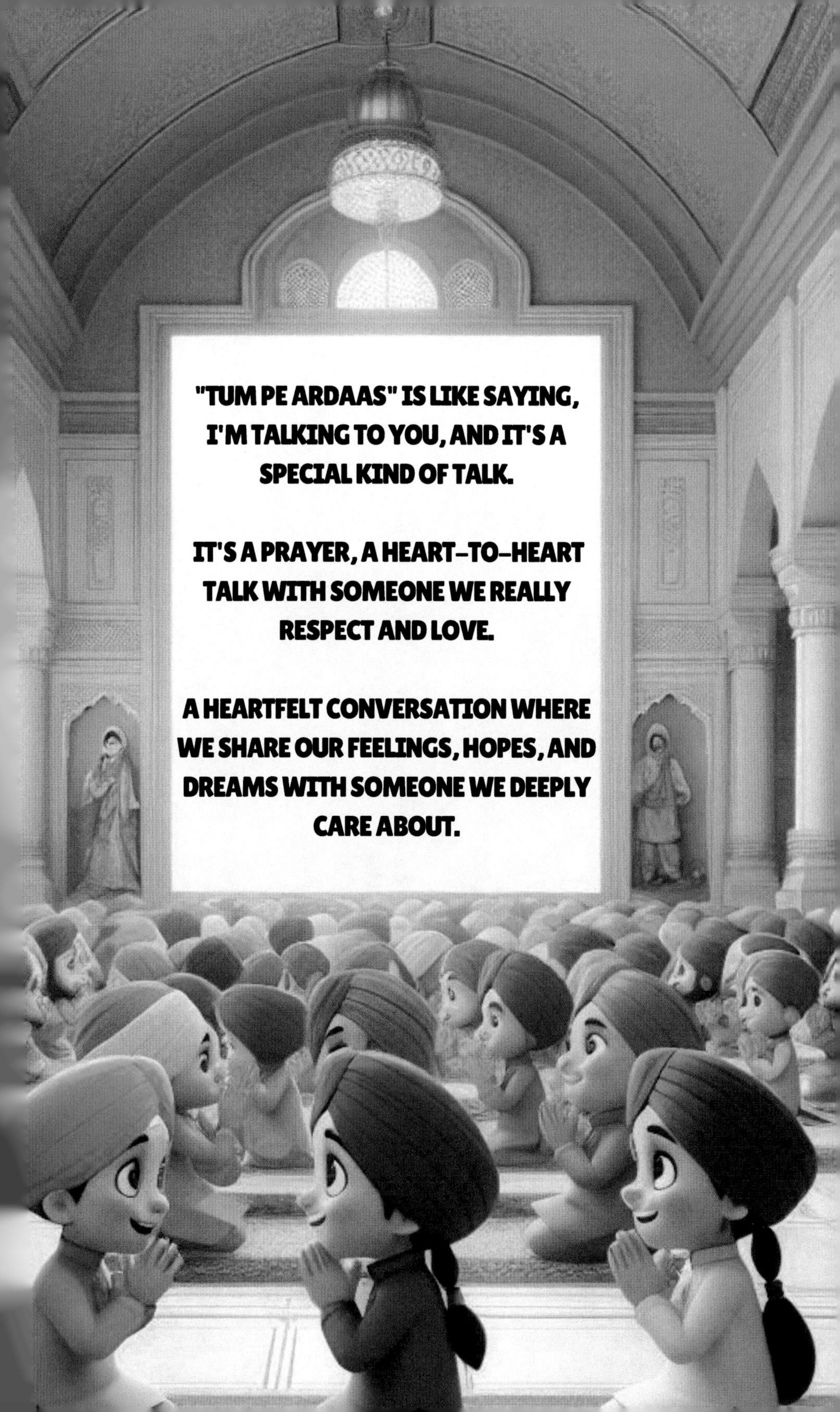
"TUM PE ARDAAS" IS LIKE SAYING, I'M TALKING TO YOU, AND IT'S A SPECIAL KIND OF TALK.
IT'S A PRAYER, A HEART-TO-HEART TALK WITH SOMEONE WE REALLY RESPECT AND LOVE.
A HEARTFELT CONVERSATION WHERE WE SHARE OUR FEELINGS, HOPES, AND DREAMS WITH SOMEONE WE DEEPLY CARE ABOUT.

ਜੀਉ ਪਿੰਡ ਸਭ

THIS BODY AND SOUL ARE ALL

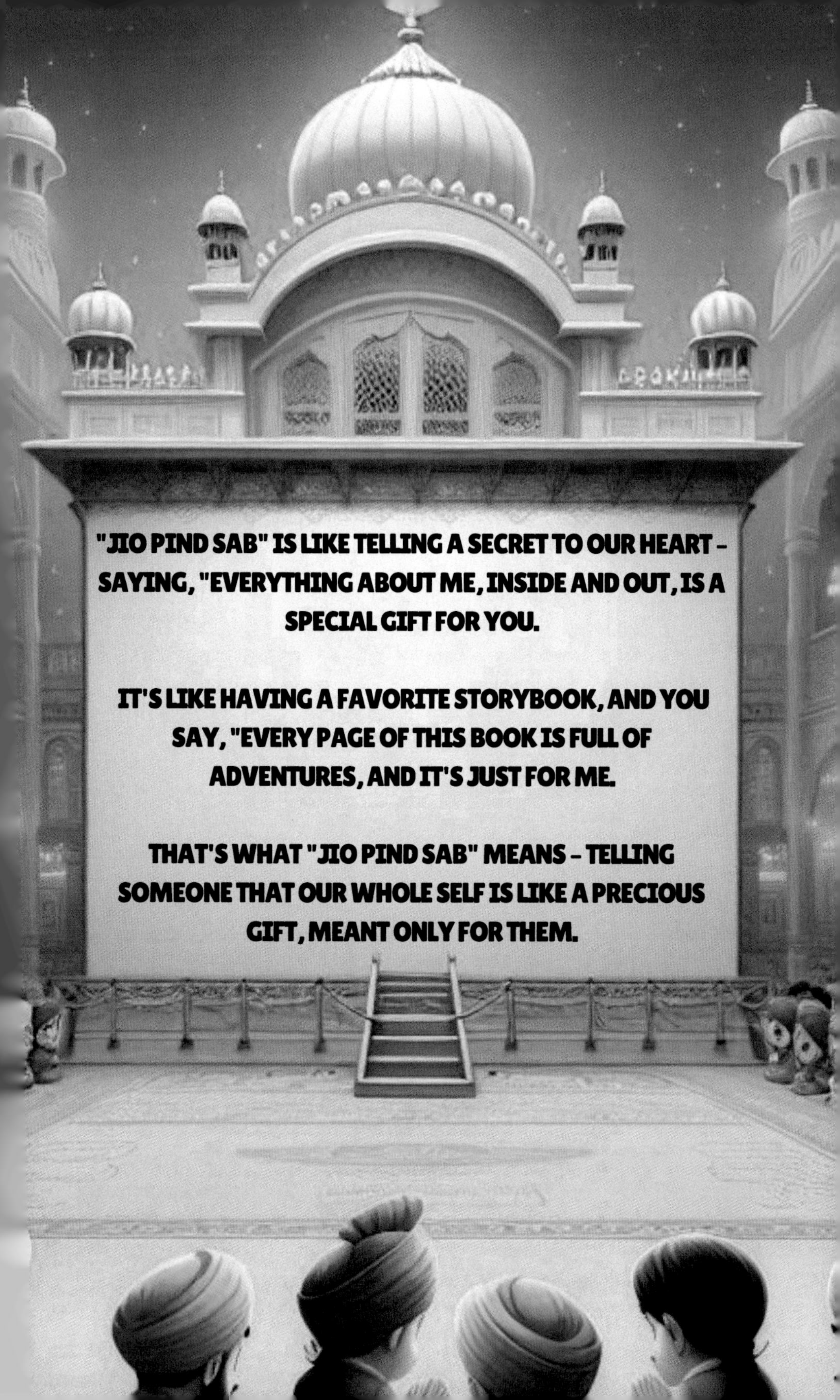
"JIO PIND SAB" IS LIKE TELLING A SECRET TO OUR HEART - SAYING, "EVERYTHING ABOUT ME, INSIDE AND OUT, IS A SPECIAL GIFT FOR YOU.

IT'S LIKE HAVING A FAVORITE STORYBOOK, AND YOU SAY, "EVERY PAGE OF THIS BOOK IS FULL OF ADVENTURES, AND IT'S JUST FOR ME.

THAT'S WHAT "JIO PIND SAB" MEANS - TELLING SOMEONE THAT OUR WHOLE SELF IS LIKE A PRECIOUS GIFT, MEANT ONLY FOR THEM.

ਤੇਰੀ ਰਾਸ

ARE ALL YOUR BELONGING

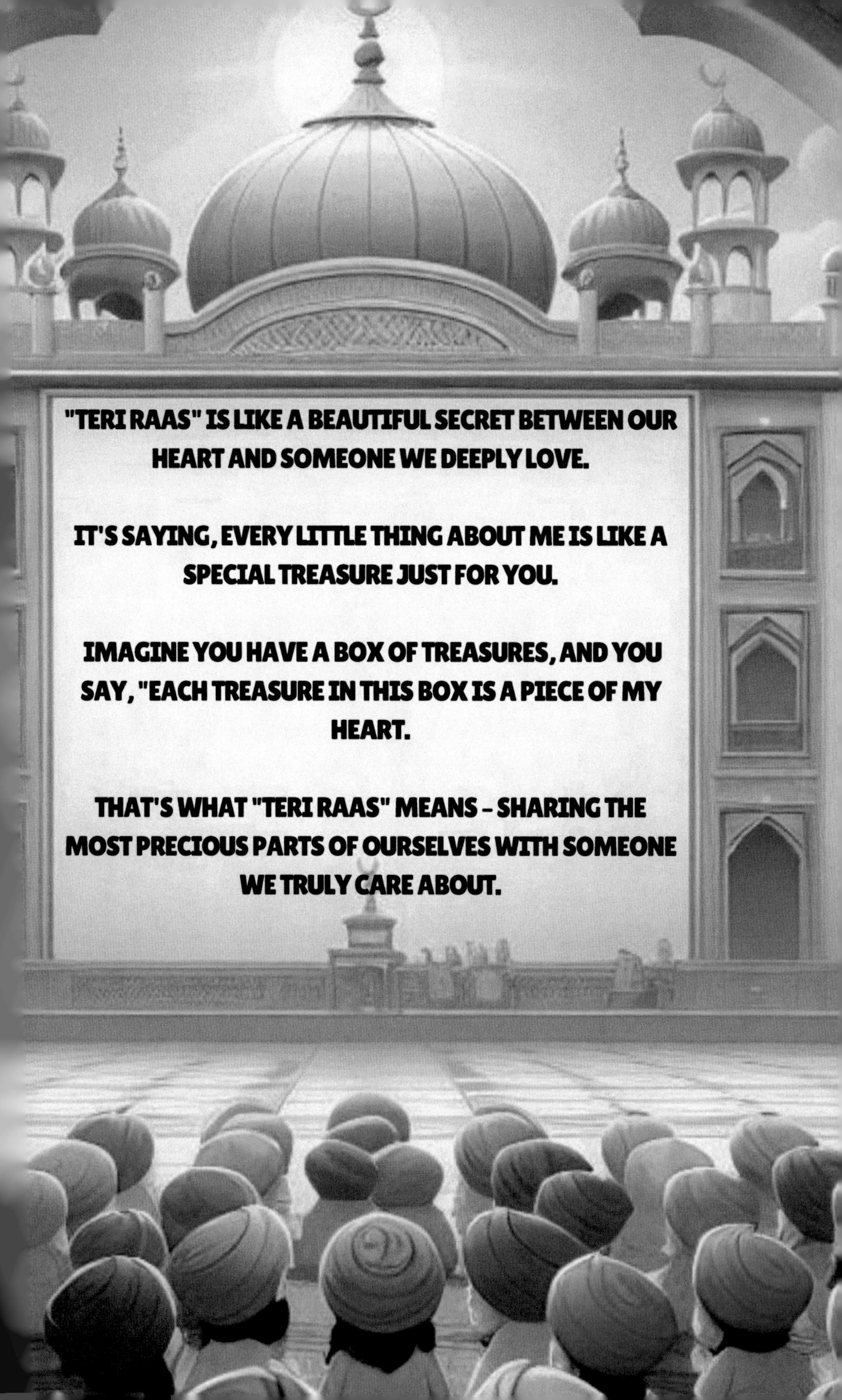
"TERI RAAS" IS LIKE A BEAUTIFUL SECRET BETWEEN OUR HEART AND SOMEONE WE DEEPLY LOVE.
IT'S SAYING, EVERY LITTLE THING ABOUT ME IS LIKE A SPECIAL TREASURE JUST FOR YOU.
IMAGINE YOU HAVE A BOX OF TREASURES, AND YOU SAY, "EACH TREASURE IN THIS BOX IS A PIECE OF MY HEART.
THAT'S WHAT "TERI RAAS" MEANS - SHARING THE MOST PRECIOUS PARTS OF OURSELVES WITH SOMEONE WE TRULY CARE ABOUT.

ਤੁਮ ਮਾਤਾ ਪਿਤਾ

YOU ARE OUR MOTHER AND FATHER

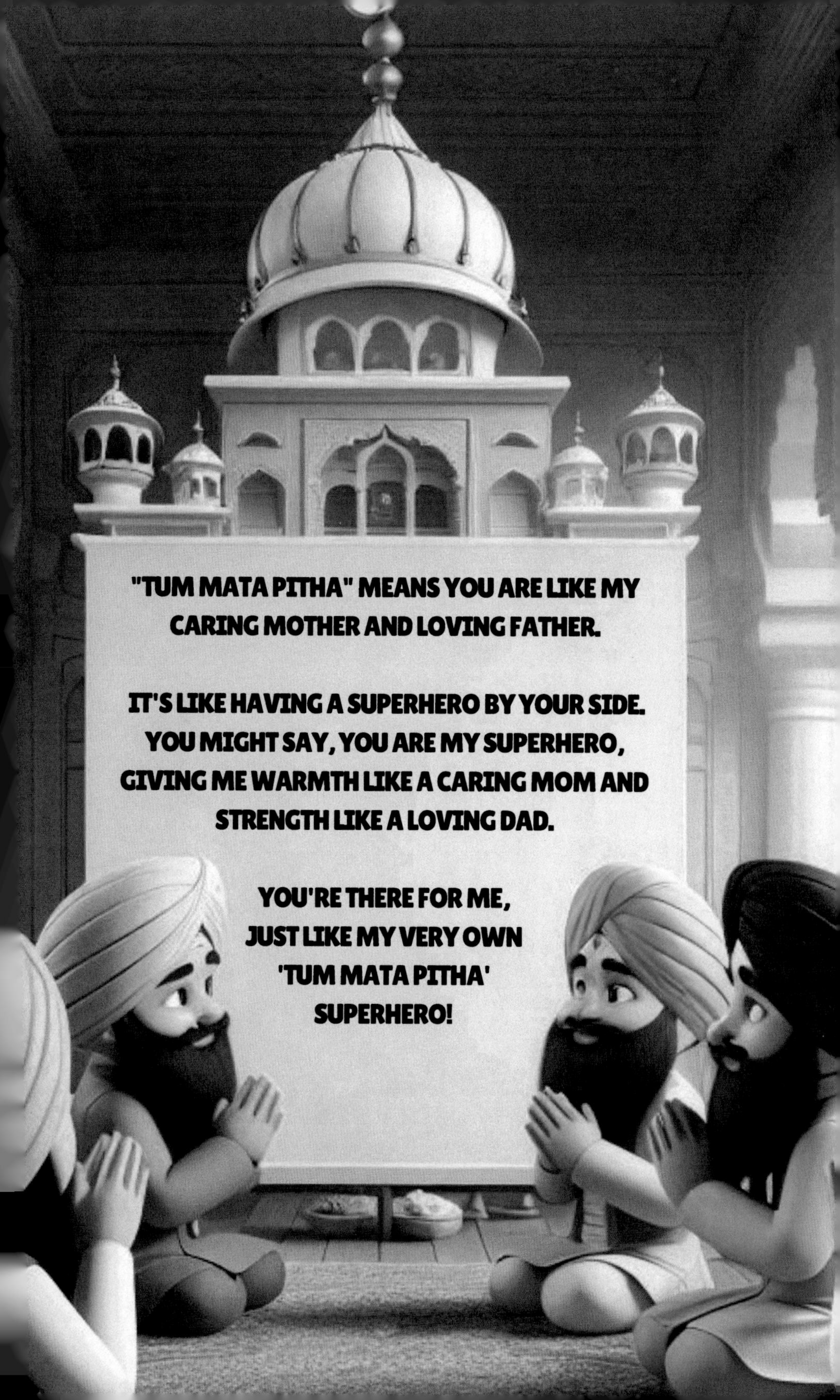

"TUM MATA PITHA" MEANS YOU ARE LIKE MY CARING MOTHER AND LOVING FATHER.

IT'S LIKE HAVING A SUPERHERO BY YOUR SIDE. YOU MIGHT SAY, YOU ARE MY SUPERHERO, GIVING ME WARMTH LIKE A CARING MOM AND STRENGTH LIKE A LOVING DAD.

YOU'RE THERE FOR ME,
JUST LIKE MY VERY OWN
'TUM MATA PITHA'
SUPERHERO!

ਹਮ ਬਾਰਿਕ ਤੇਰੇ

AND WE ARE YOUR CHILDREN

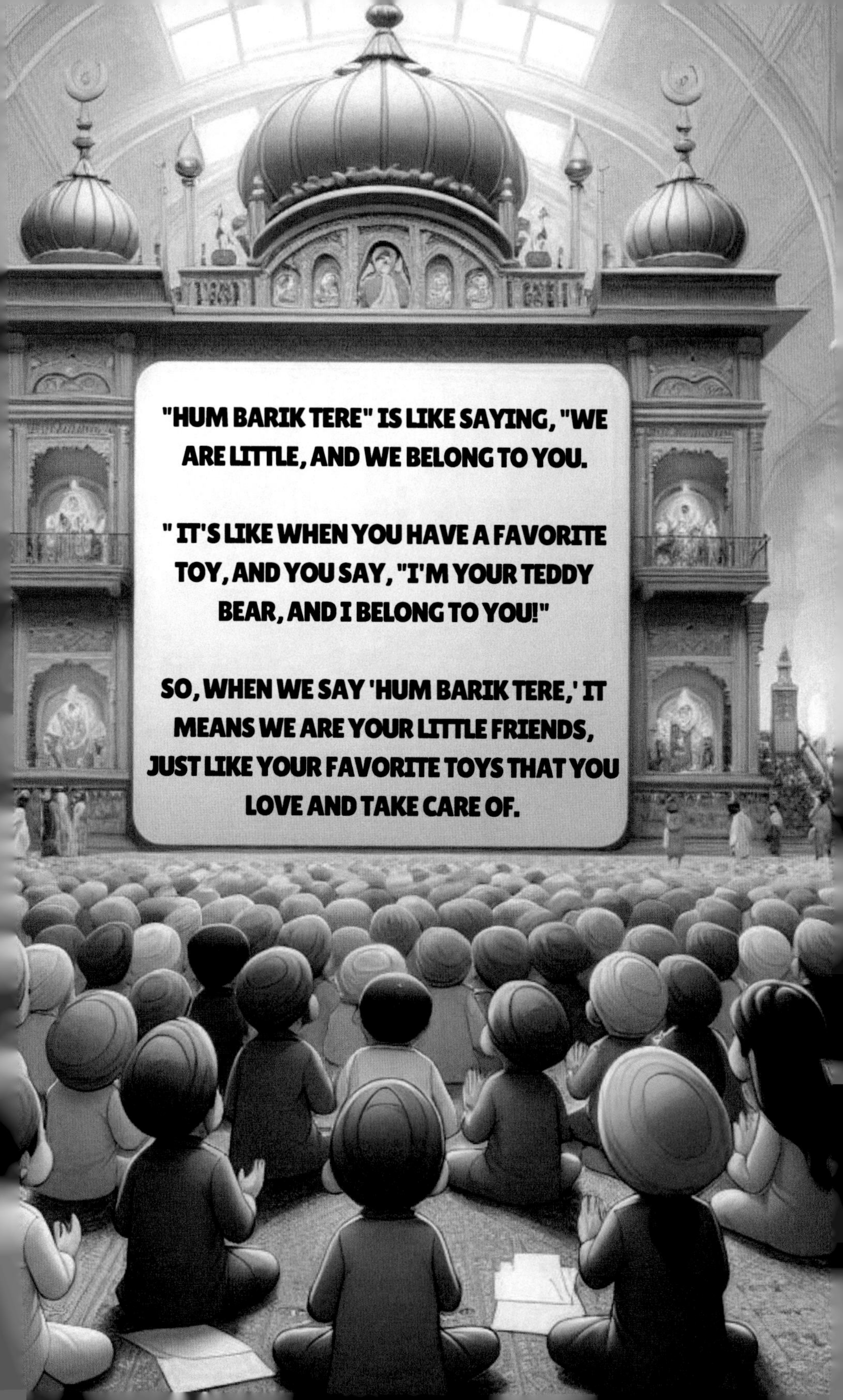
"HUM BARIK TERE" IS LIKE SAYING, "WE ARE LITTLE, AND WE BELONG TO YOU.
" IT'S LIKE WHEN YOU HAVE A FAVORITE TOY, AND YOU SAY, "I'M YOUR TEDDY BEAR, AND I BELONG TO YOU!"
SO, WHEN WE SAY 'HUM BARIK TERE,' IT MEANS WE ARE YOUR LITTLE FRIENDS, JUST LIKE YOUR FAVORITE TOYS THAT YOU LOVE AND TAKE CARE OF.

ਤੁਮਰੀ ਕਿਰਪਾ

IN YOUR GRACE

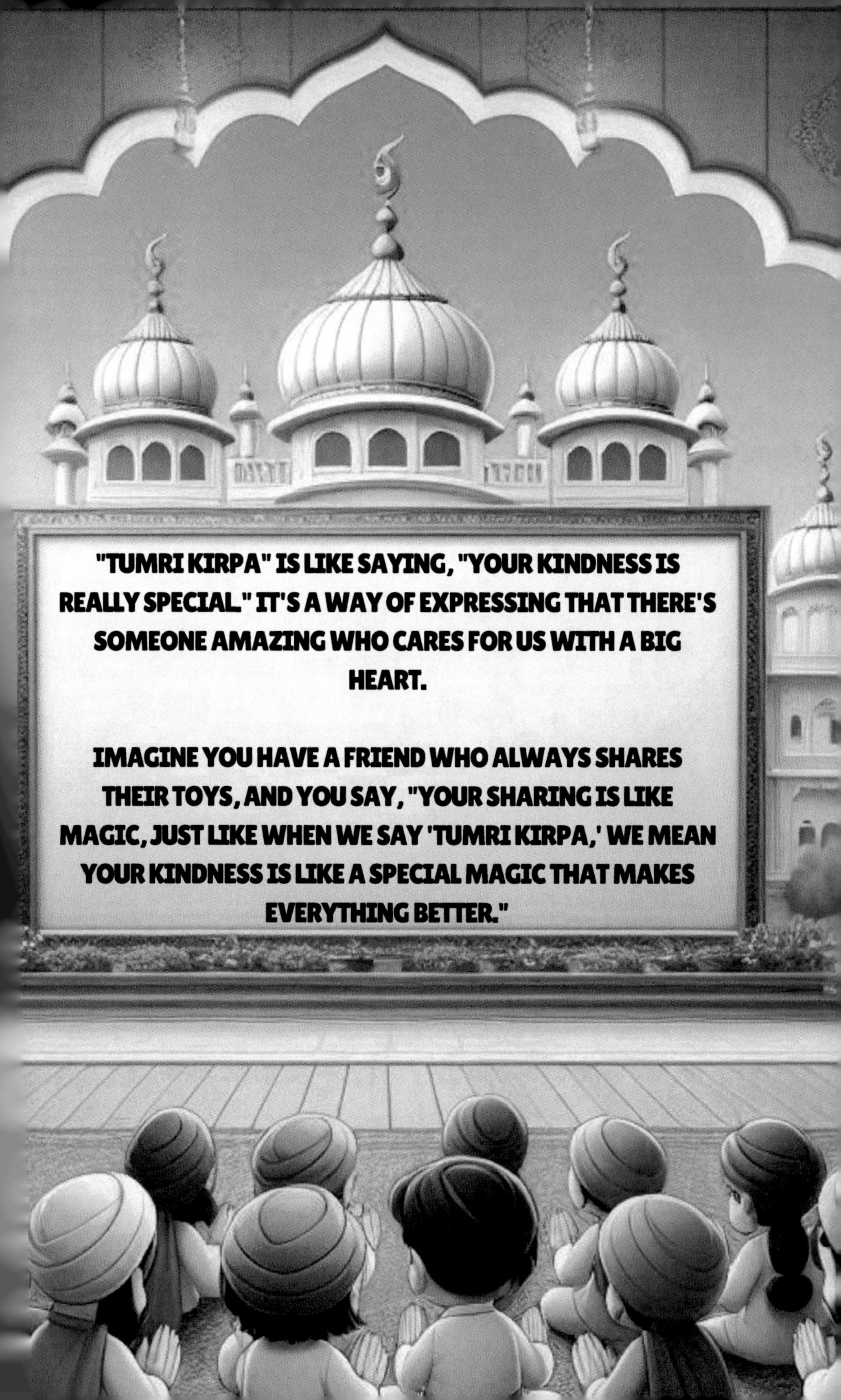
"TUMRI KIRPA" IS LIKE SAYING, "YOUR KINDNESS IS REALLY SPECIAL." IT'S A WAY OF EXPRESSING THAT THERE'S SOMEONE AMAZING WHO CARES FOR US WITH A BIG HEART.
IMAGINE YOU HAVE A FRIEND WHO ALWAYS SHARES THEIR TOYS, AND YOU SAY, "YOUR SHARING IS LIKE MAGIC, JUST LIKE WHEN WE SAY 'TUMRI KIRPA,' WE MEAN YOUR KINDNESS IS LIKE A SPECIAL MAGIC THAT MAKES EVERYTHING BETTER."

MEH SUKH GHANERRE

ਮੈਂ ਸੁਖ ਘਣੇਰੇ

WE EXPERIENCE ULTIMATE PEACE

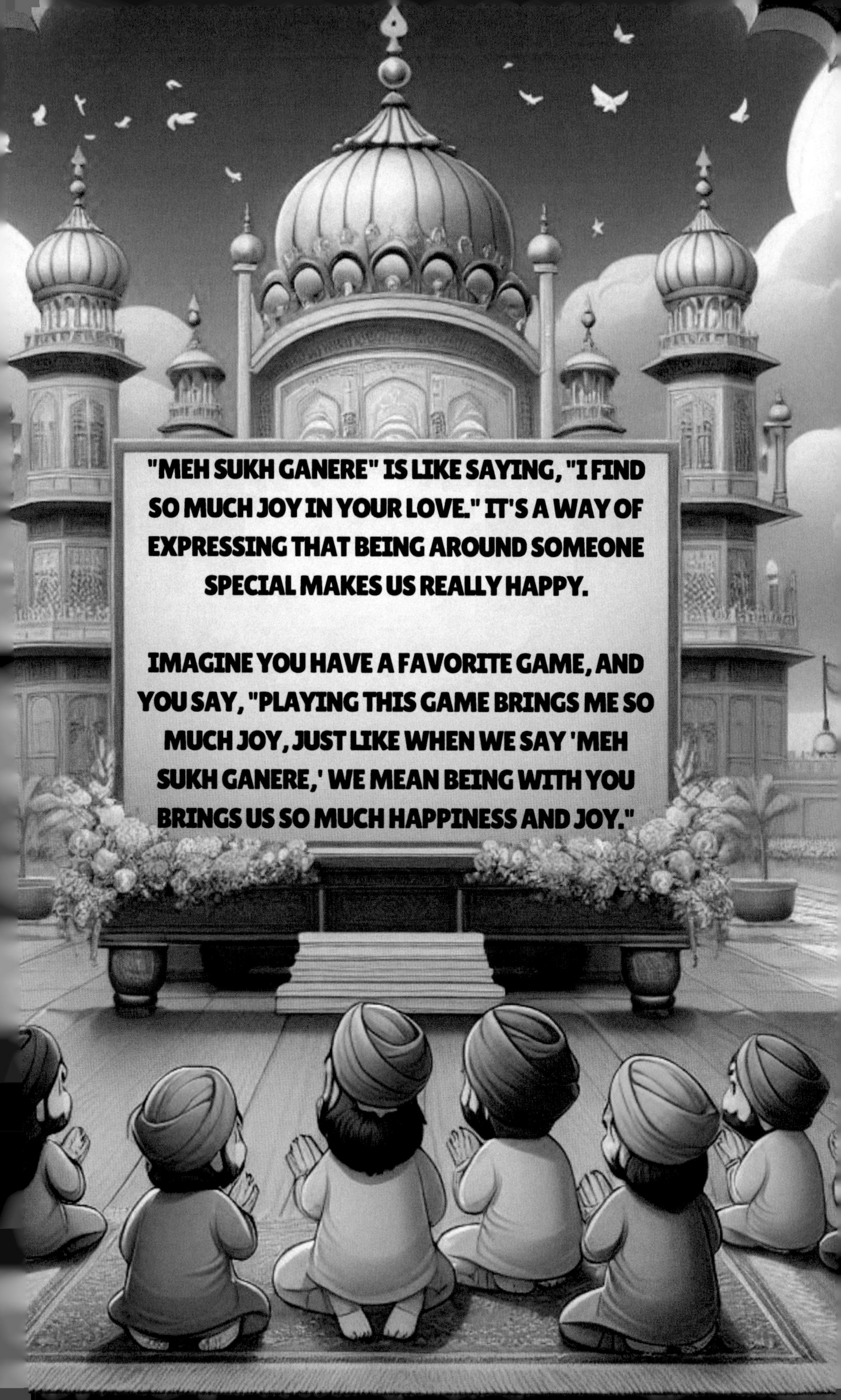
"MEH SUKH GANERE" IS LIKE SAYING, "I FIND SO MUCH JOY IN YOUR LOVE." IT'S A WAY OF EXPRESSING THAT BEING AROUND SOMEONE SPECIAL MAKES US REALLY HAPPY.
IMAGINE YOU HAVE A FAVORITE GAME, AND YOU SAY, "PLAYING THIS GAME BRINGS ME SO MUCH JOY, JUST LIKE WHEN WE SAY 'MEH SUKH GANERE,' WE MEAN BEING WITH YOU BRINGS US SO MUCH HAPPINESS AND JOY."

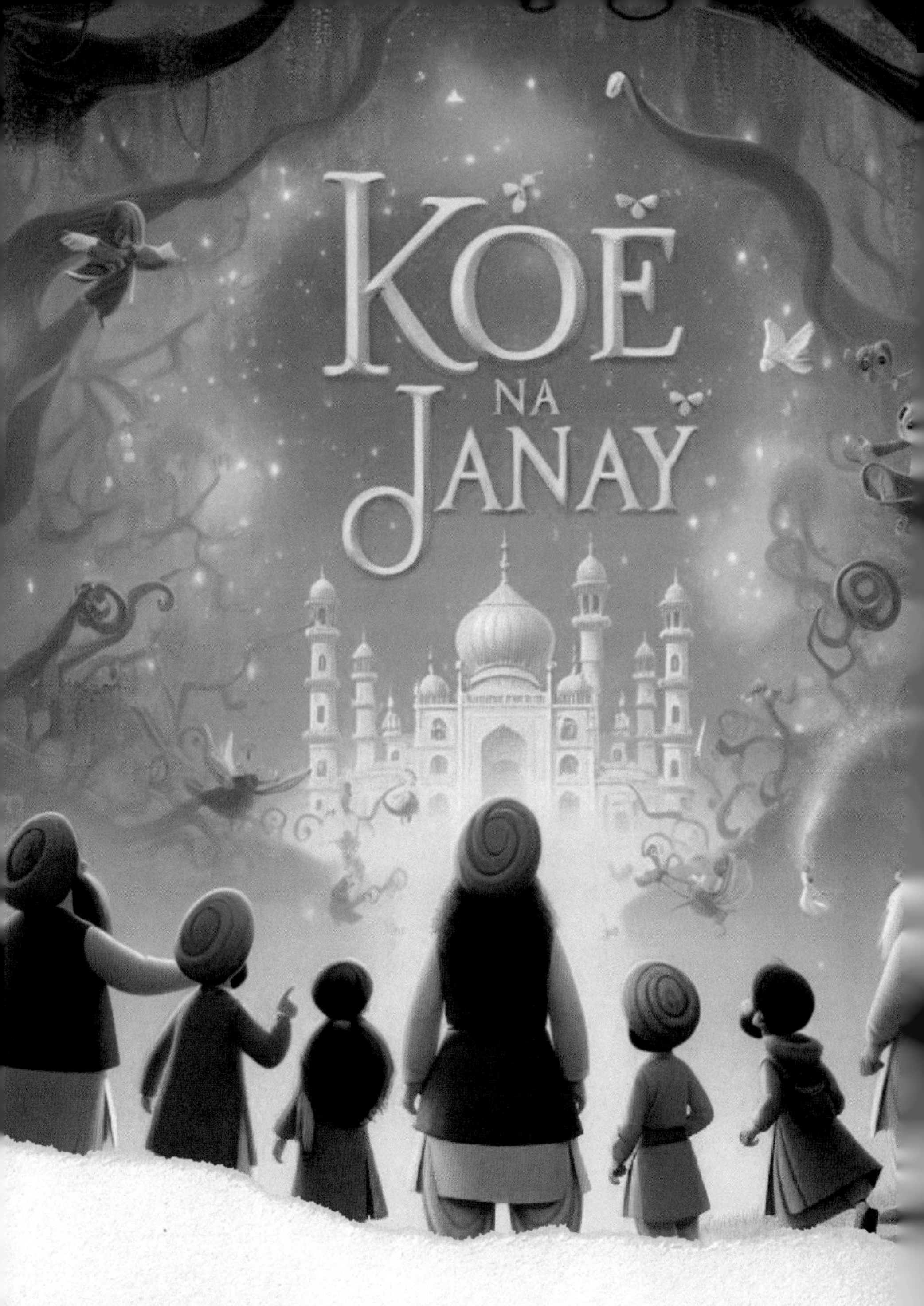

ਕੋਇ ਨਾ ਜਾਨੈ

NO-ONE KNOWS

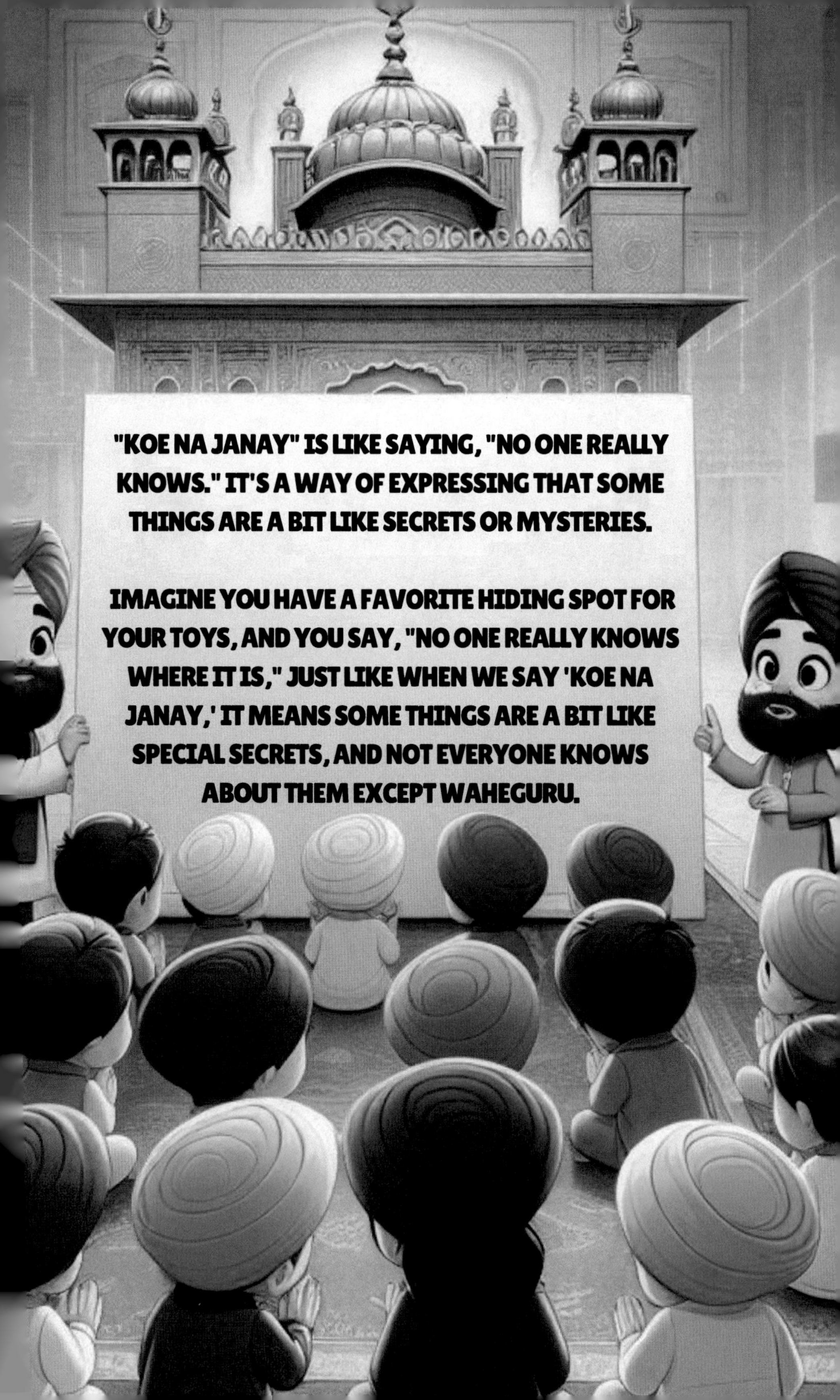
"KOE NA JANAY" IS LIKE SAYING, "NO ONE REALLY KNOWS." IT'S A WAY OF EXPRESSING THAT SOME THINGS ARE A BIT LIKE SECRETS OR MYSTERIES.

IMAGINE YOU HAVE A FAVORITE HIDING SPOT FOR YOUR TOYS, AND YOU SAY, "NO ONE REALLY KNOWS WHERE IT IS," JUST LIKE WHEN WE SAY 'KOE NA JANAY,' IT MEANS SOME THINGS ARE A BIT LIKE SPECIAL SECRETS, AND NOT EVERYONE KNOWS ABOUT THEM EXCEPT WAHEGURU.

ਤੁਮਰਾ ਅੰਤ

YOUR INFINITE VASTNESS

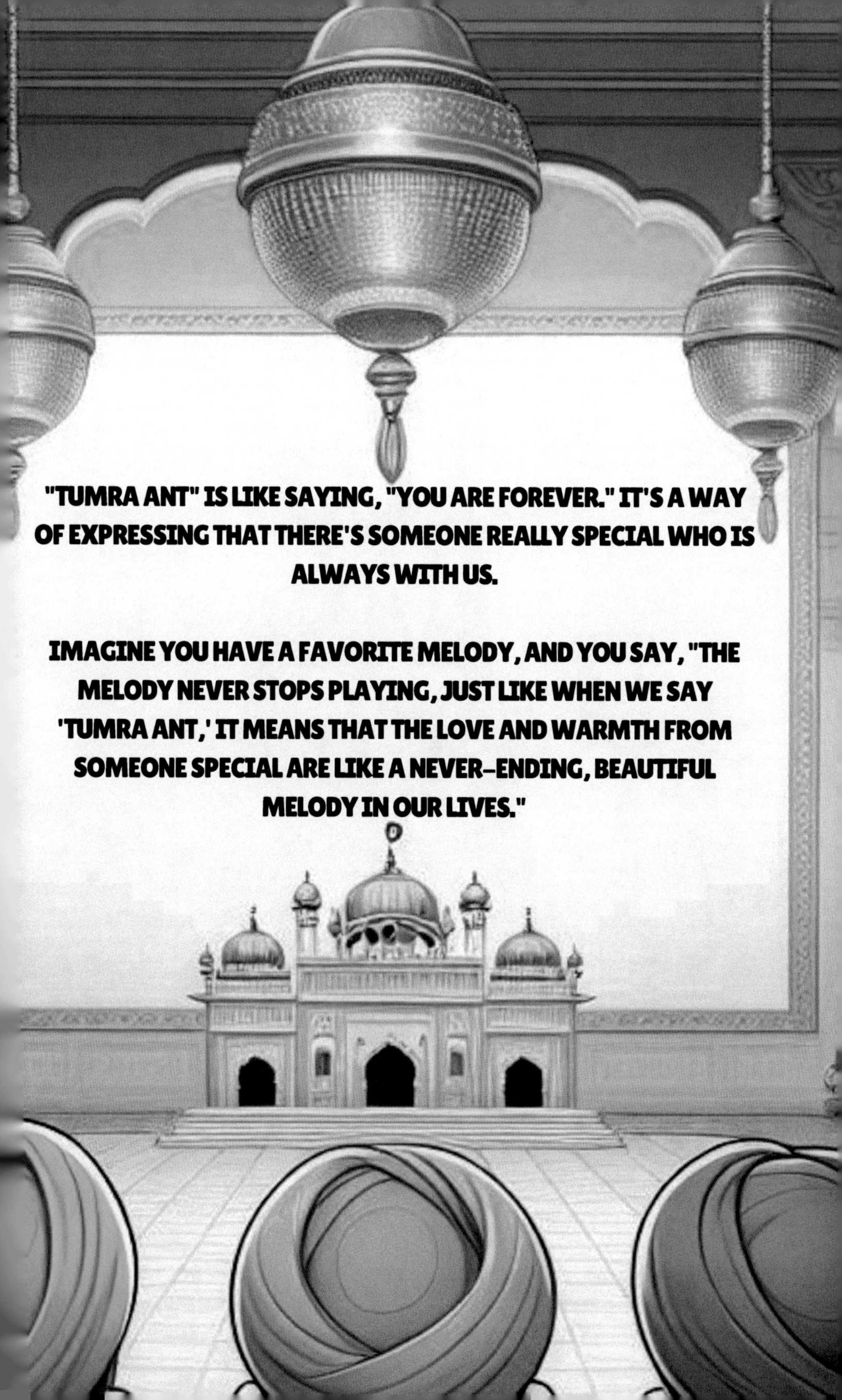

"TUMRA ANT" IS LIKE SAYING, "YOU ARE FOREVER." IT'S A WAY OF EXPRESSING THAT THERE'S SOMEONE REALLY SPECIAL WHO IS ALWAYS WITH US.

IMAGINE YOU HAVE A FAVORITE MELODY, AND YOU SAY, "THE MELODY NEVER STOPS PLAYING, JUST LIKE WHEN WE SAY 'TUMRA ANT,' IT MEANS THAT THE LOVE AND WARMTH FROM SOMEONE SPECIAL ARE LIKE A NEVER-ENDING, BEAUTIFUL MELODY IN OUR LIVES."

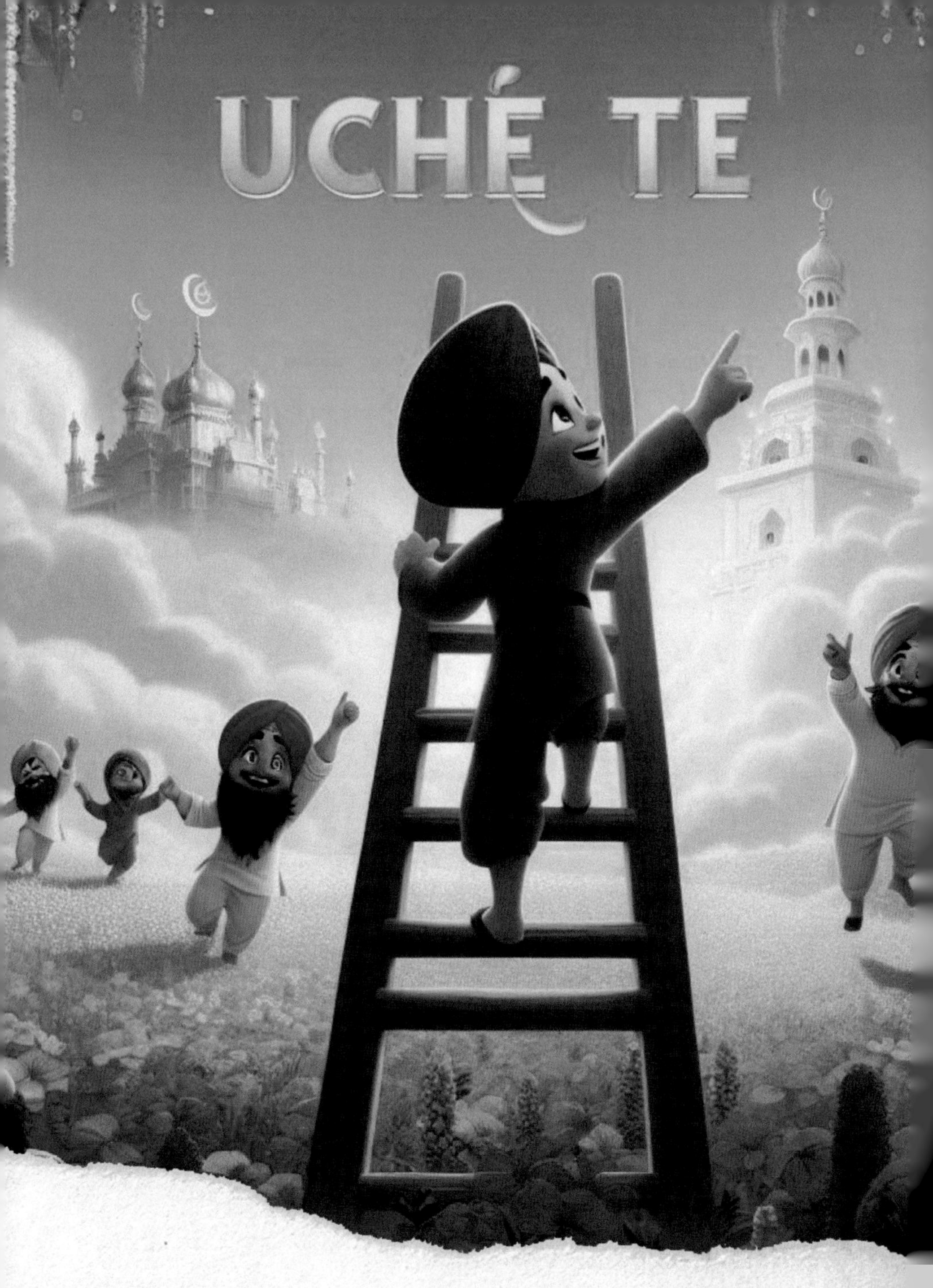

ਊਚੇ ਤੇ

O HIGHEST OF THE HIGH

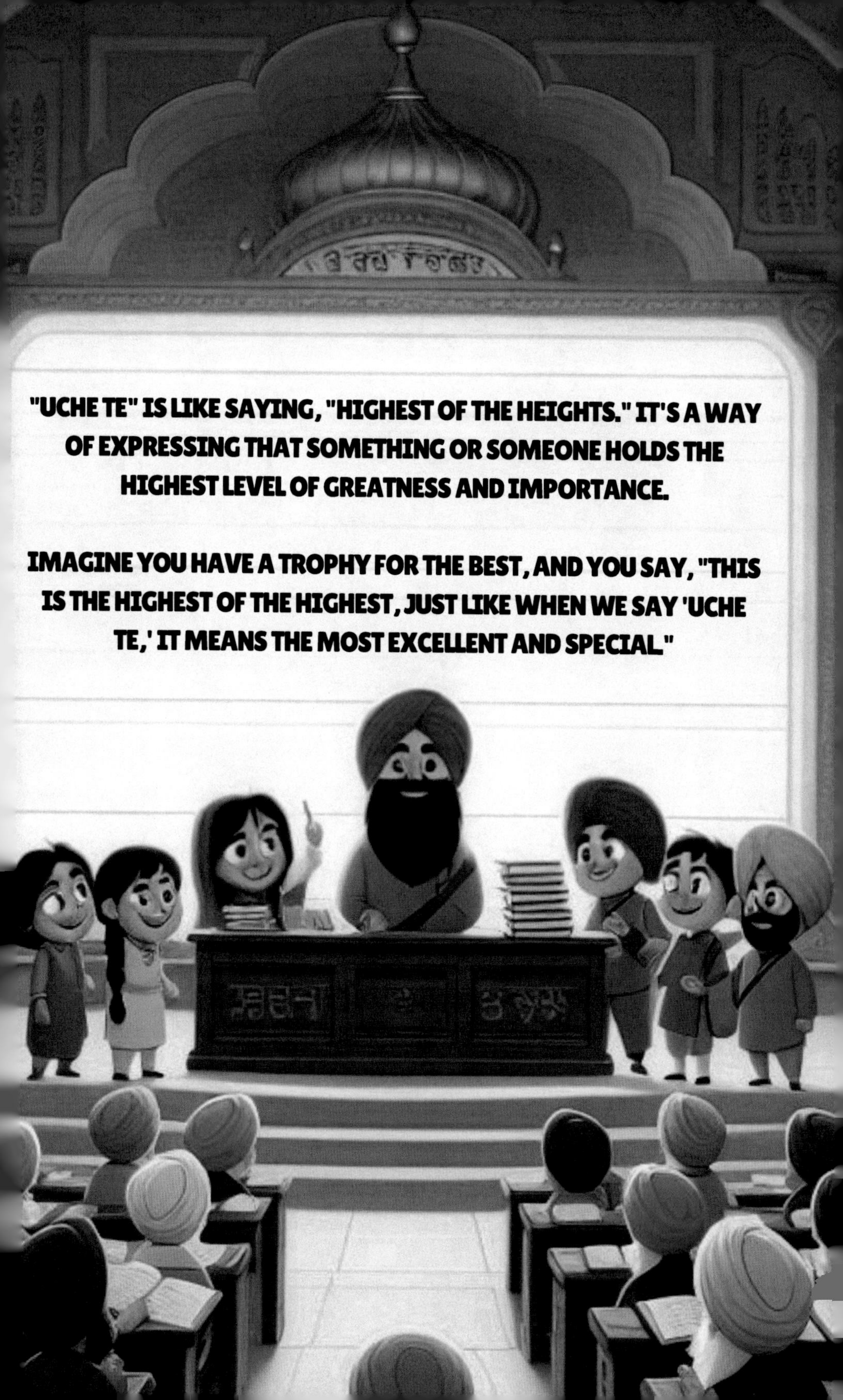

"UCHE TE" IS LIKE SAYING, "HIGHEST OF THE HEIGHTS." IT'S A WAY OF EXPRESSING THAT SOMETHING OR SOMEONE HOLDS THE HIGHEST LEVEL OF GREATNESS AND IMPORTANCE.

IMAGINE YOU HAVE A TROPHY FOR THE BEST, AND YOU SAY, "THIS IS THE HIGHEST OF THE HIGHEST, JUST LIKE WHEN WE SAY 'UCHE TE,' IT MEANS THE MOST EXCELLENT AND SPECIAL."

ਊਚਾ ਭਗਵੰਤ

MOST GENEROUS GOD

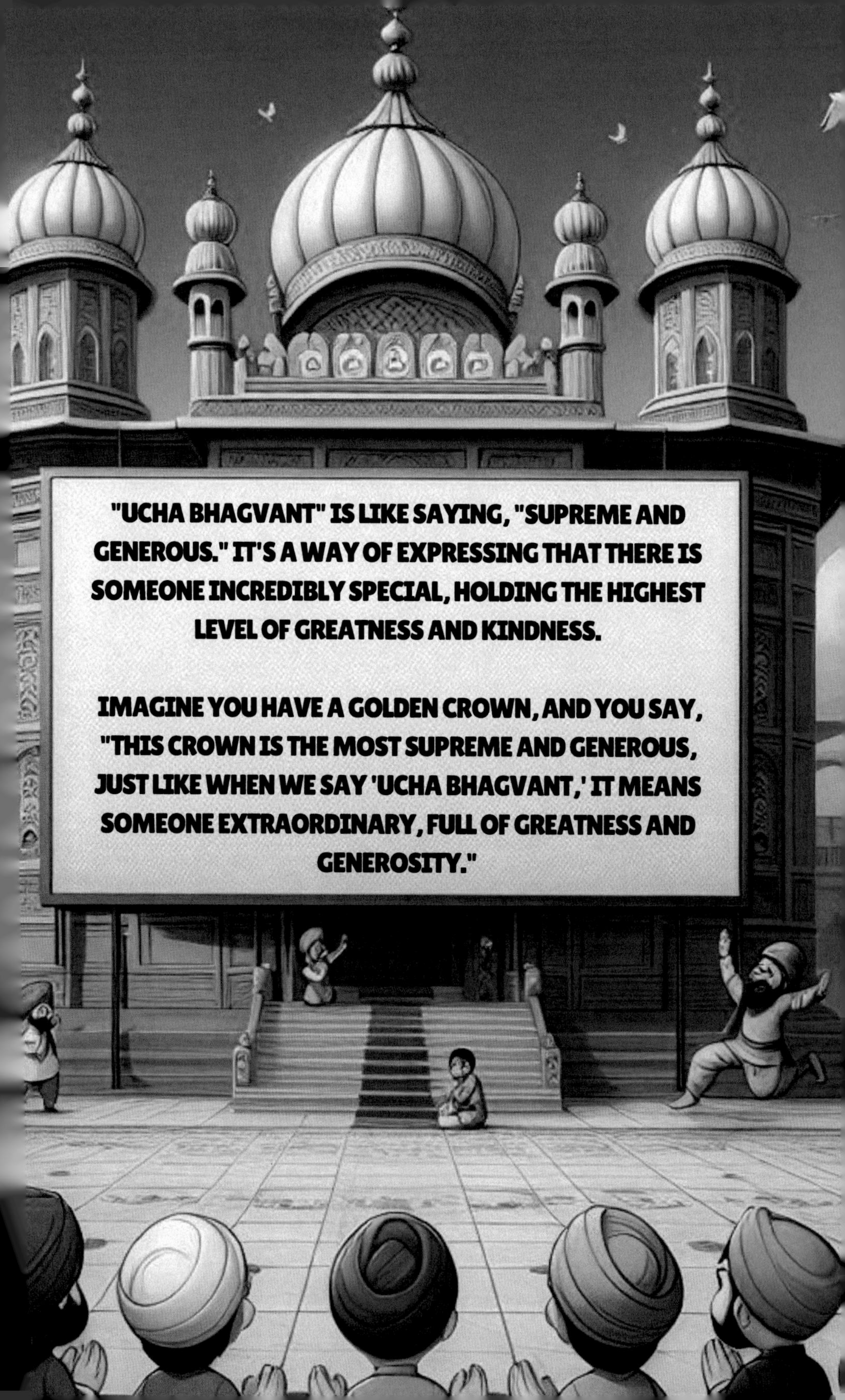
"UCHA BHAGVANT" IS LIKE SAYING, "SUPREME AND GENEROUS." IT'S A WAY OF EXPRESSING THAT THERE IS SOMEONE INCREDIBLY SPECIAL, HOLDING THE HIGHEST LEVEL OF GREATNESS AND KINDNESS.
IMAGINE YOU HAVE A GOLDEN CROWN, AND YOU SAY, "THIS CROWN IS THE MOST SUPREME AND GENEROUS, JUST LIKE WHEN WE SAY 'UCHA BHAGVANT,' IT MEANS SOMEONE EXTRAORDINARY, FULL OF GREATNESS AND GENEROSITY."

ਸਗਲ ਸਮਗਰੀ

THE WHOLE CREATION

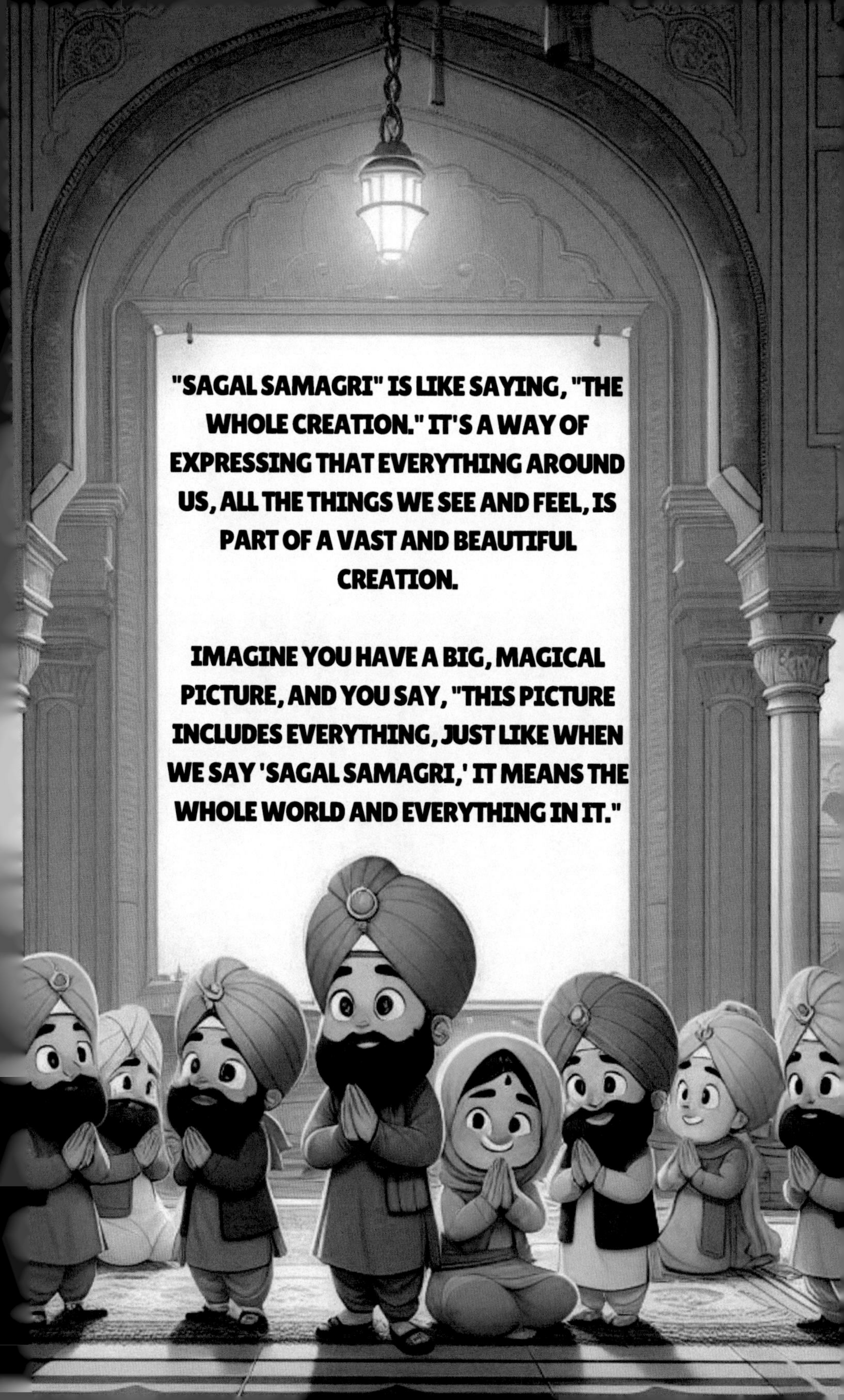

"SAGAL SAMAGRI" IS LIKE SAYING, "THE WHOLE CREATION." IT'S A WAY OF EXPRESSING THAT EVERYTHING AROUND US, ALL THE THINGS WE SEE AND FEEL, IS PART OF A VAST AND BEAUTIFUL CREATION.

IMAGINE YOU HAVE A BIG, MAGICAL PICTURE, AND YOU SAY, "THIS PICTURE INCLUDES EVERYTHING, JUST LIKE WHEN WE SAY 'SAGAL SAMAGRI,' IT MEANS THE WHOLE WORLD AND EVERYTHING IN IT."

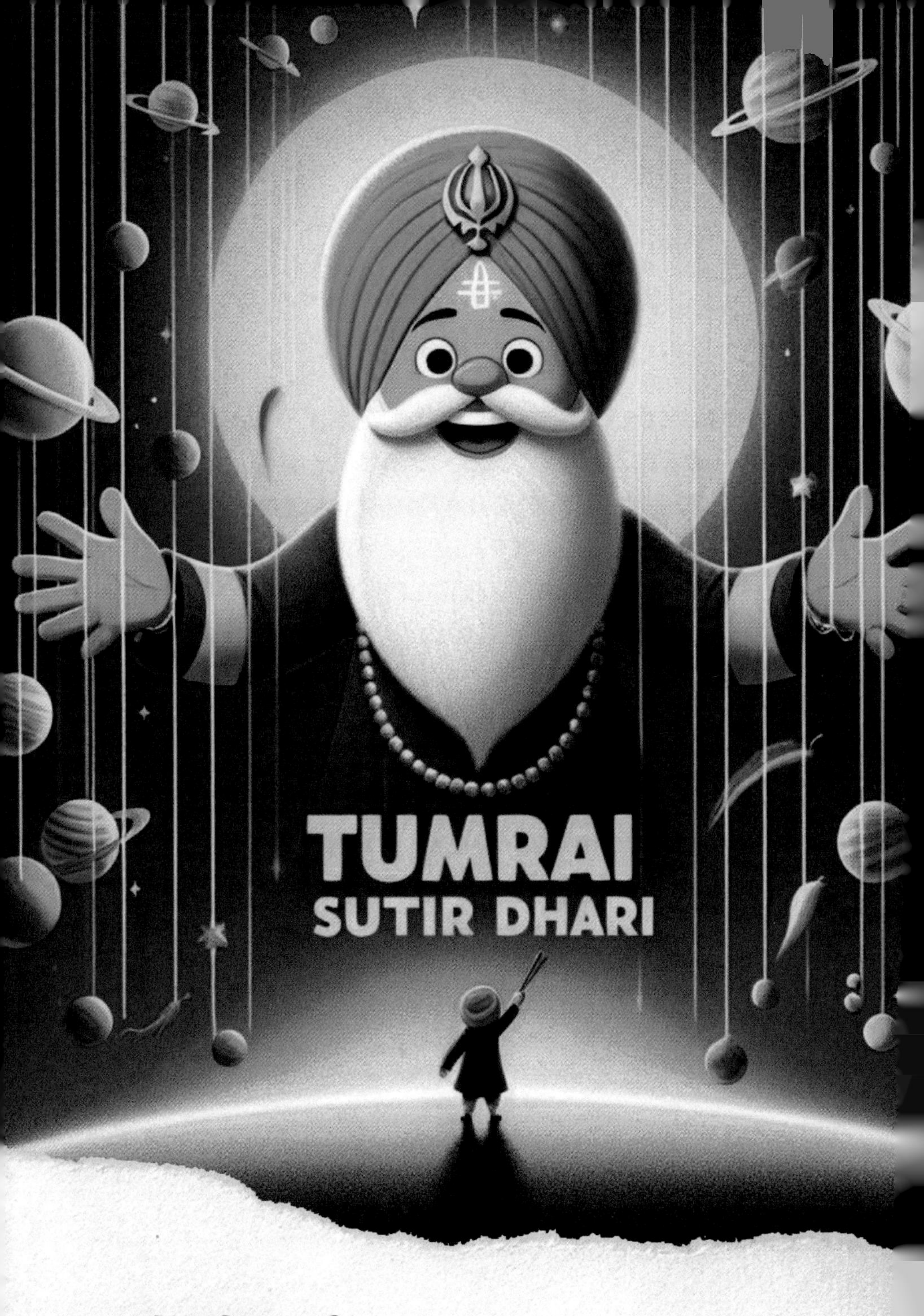

ਤੁਮਰੈ ਸੂਤ੍ਰਿ ਧਾਰੀ

IS STRUNG ON YOUR THREAD

"TUMRE SUTIR DHARI" IS LIKE SAYING, "STRUNG ON YOUR THREAD." IT'S A WAY OF EXPRESSING THAT EVERYTHING IN THE WORLD IS CONNECTED AND HELD TOGETHER BY SOMETHING SPECIAL.
IMAGINE YOU HAVE A STRING WEAVING THROUGH YOUR FAVORITE BEADS, AND YOU SAY, "THIS STRING HOLDS EVERYTHING TOGETHER, JUST LIKE WHEN WE SAY 'TUMRE SUTIR DHARI,' IT MEANS EVERYTHING IN THE WORLD IS CONNECTED BY A SPECIAL THREAD."

ਤੁਮ ਤੇ ਹੋਇ

THAT WHICH HAS COME FROM YOU

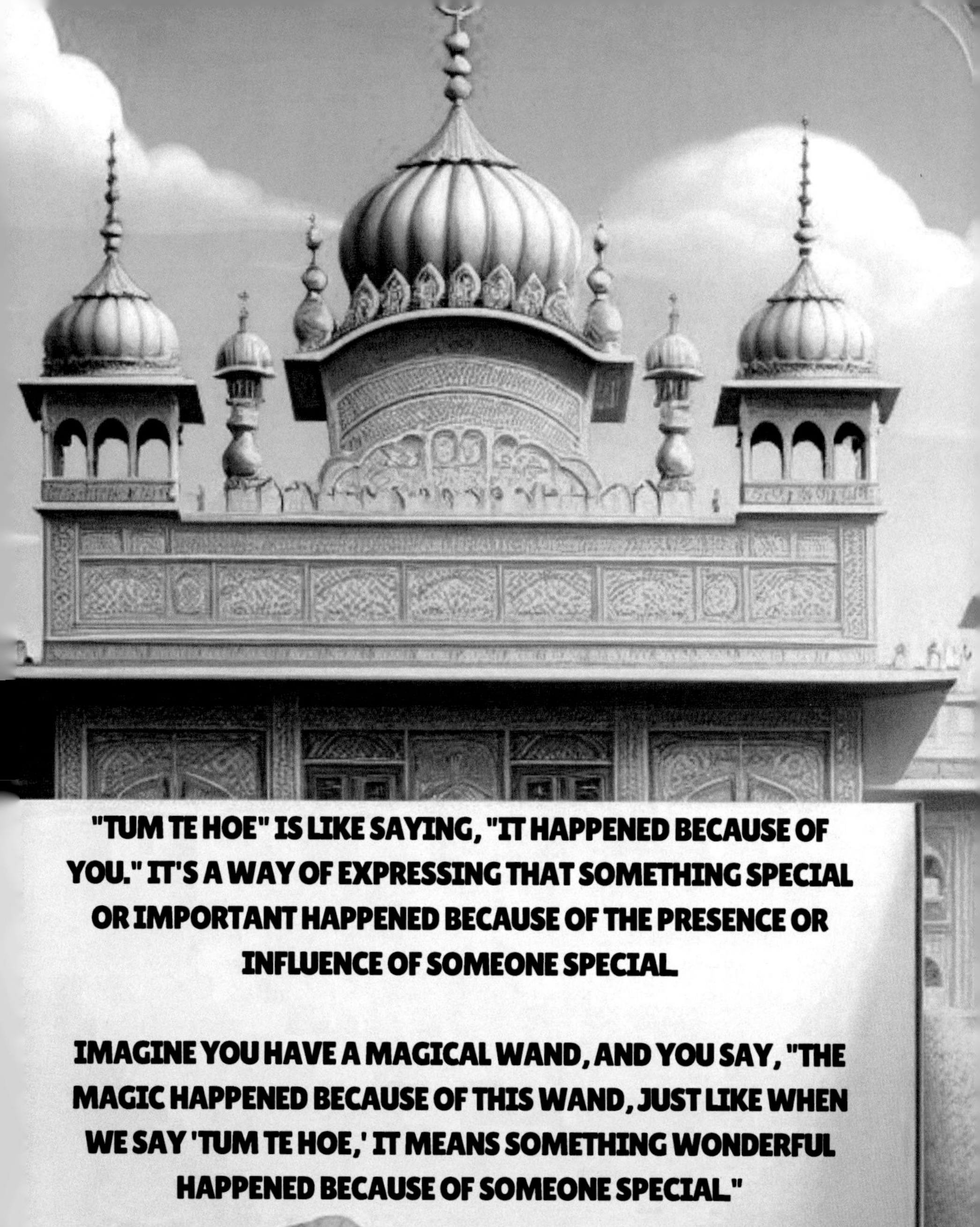

"TUM TE HOE" IS LIKE SAYING, "IT HAPPENED BECAUSE OF YOU." IT'S A WAY OF EXPRESSING THAT SOMETHING SPECIAL OR IMPORTANT HAPPENED BECAUSE OF THE PRESENCE OR INFLUENCE OF SOMEONE SPECIAL.

IMAGINE YOU HAVE A MAGICAL WAND, AND YOU SAY, "THE MAGIC HAPPENED BECAUSE OF THIS WAND, JUST LIKE WHEN WE SAY 'TUM TE HOE,' IT MEANS SOMETHING WONDERFUL HAPPENED BECAUSE OF SOMEONE SPECIAL."

ਸੁ ਆਗਿਆਕਾਰੀ

IS IN YOUR WILL

"SO AGIAKARI" IS LIKE SAYING, "OBEDIENT TO YOUR WILL." IT'S A WAY OF EXPRESSING THAT SOMEONE IS LISTENING AND FOLLOWING THE GUIDANCE AND WISHES OF SOMEONE SPECIAL.

IMAGINE YOU HAVE A TRUSTED GUIDE, AND YOU SAY, "I LISTEN AND FOLLOW THEIR ADVICE, JUST LIKE WHEN WE SAY 'SO AGIAKARI,' IT MEANS BEING OBEDIENT AND FOLLOWING THE WISE GUIDANCE OF SOMEONE SPECIAL."

ਤੁਮਰੀ ਗਤਿ ਮਿਤਿ

YOUR EXISTENCE AND VASTNESS

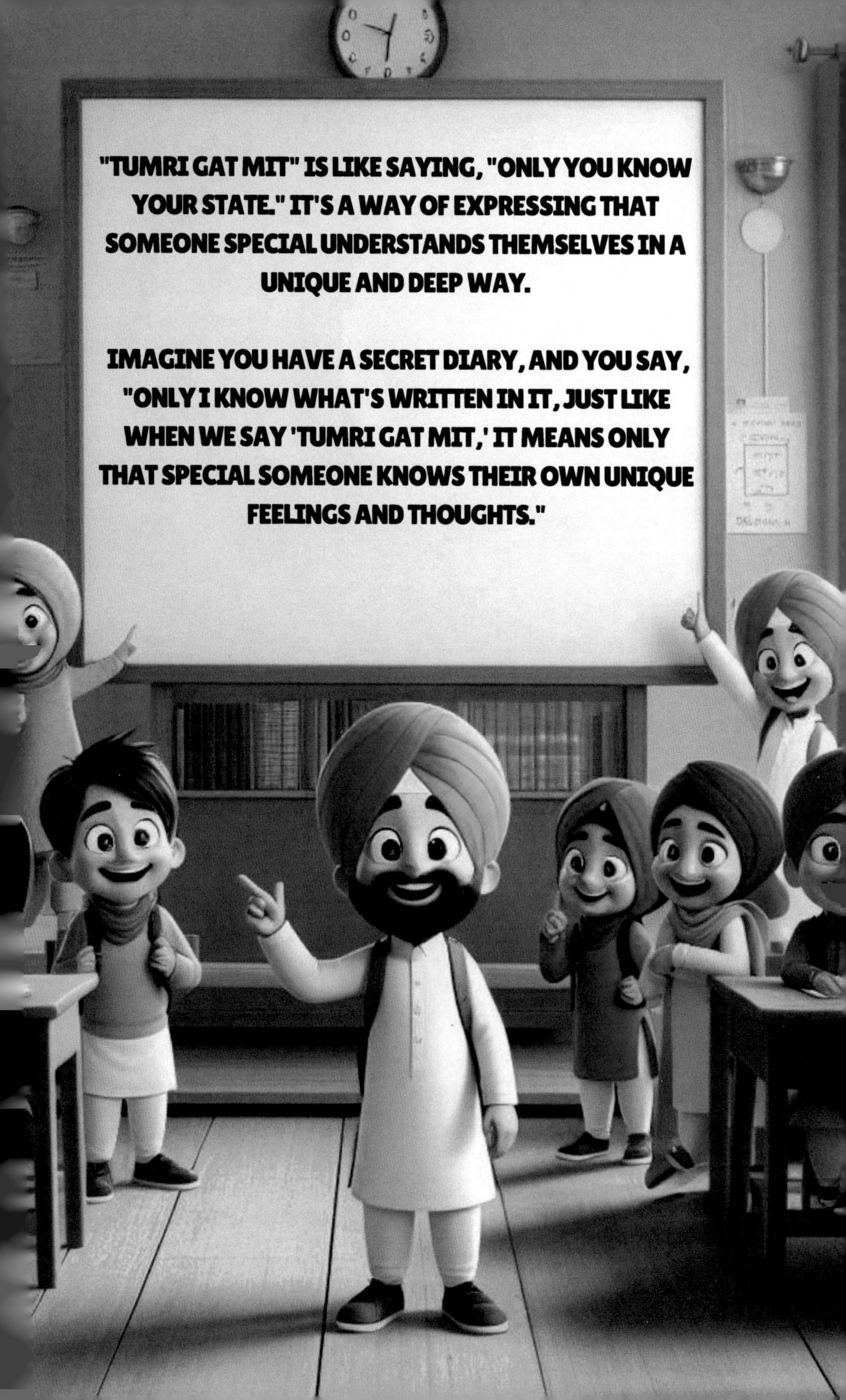
"TUMRI GAT MIT" IS LIKE SAYING, "ONLY YOU KNOW YOUR STATE." IT'S A WAY OF EXPRESSING THAT SOMEONE SPECIAL UNDERSTANDS THEMSELVES IN A UNIQUE AND DEEP WAY.
IMAGINE YOU HAVE A SECRET DIARY, AND YOU SAY, "ONLY I KNOW WHAT'S WRITTEN IN IT, JUST LIKE WHEN WE SAY 'TUMRI GAT MIT,' IT MEANS ONLY THAT SPECIAL SOMEONE KNOWS THEIR OWN UNIQUE FEELINGS AND THOUGHTS."

ਤੁਮ ਹੀ ਜਾਨੀ

ONLY YOU ALONE KNOW

"TUM HI JANI" IS LIKE SAYING, "ONLY YOU KNOW." IT'S A WAY OF EXPRESSING THAT SOMEONE SPECIAL HAS A DEEP UNDERSTANDING OR KNOWLEDGE ABOUT A PARTICULAR THING.
IMAGINE YOU HAVE A MYSTERY BOX, AND YOU SAY, "ONLY I KNOW WHAT'S INSIDE, JUST LIKE WHEN WE SAY 'TUM HI JANI,' IT MEANS ONLY THAT SPECIAL SOMEONE KNOWS ABOUT THIS PARTICULAR THING."

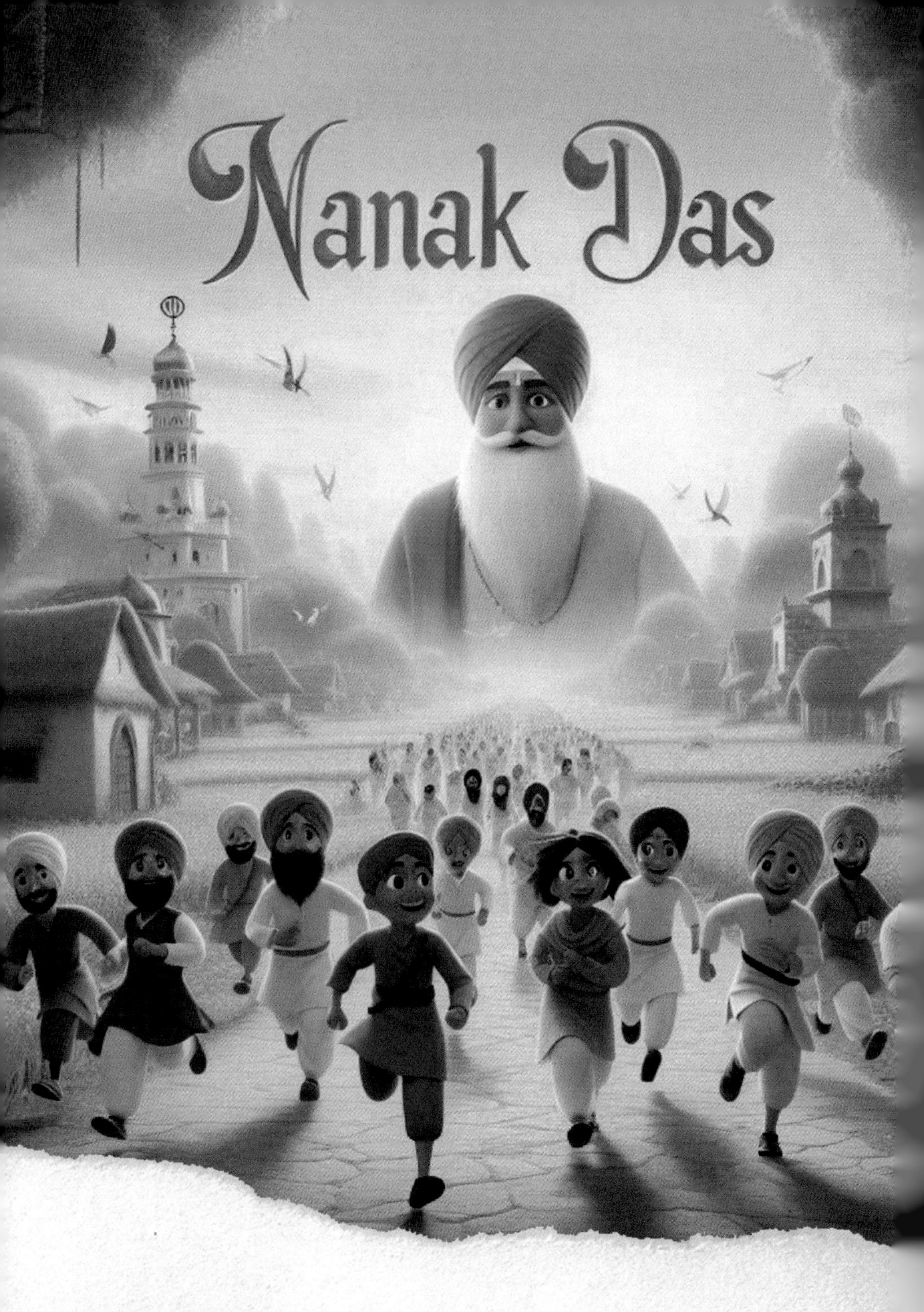

ਨਾਨਕ ਦਾਸ

NANAK, YOUR SLAVE

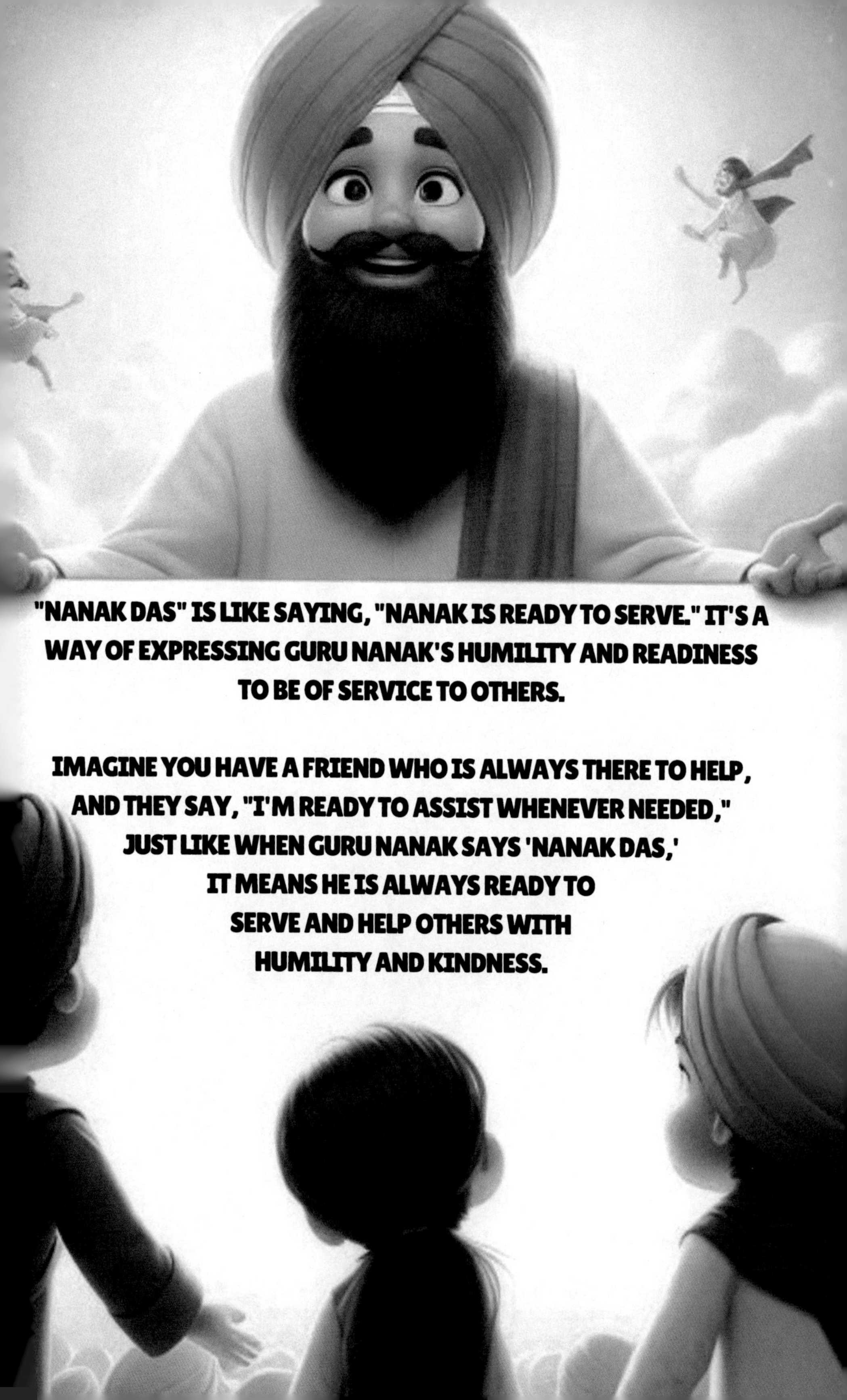

"NANAK DAS" IS LIKE SAYING, "NANAK IS READY TO SERVE." IT'S A WAY OF EXPRESSING GURU NANAK'S HUMILITY AND READINESS TO BE OF SERVICE TO OTHERS.

IMAGINE YOU HAVE A FRIEND WHO IS ALWAYS THERE TO HELP, AND THEY SAY, "I'M READY TO ASSIST WHENEVER NEEDED," JUST LIKE WHEN GURU NANAK SAYS 'NANAK DAS,' IT MEANS HE IS ALWAYS READY TO SERVE AND HELP OTHERS WITH HUMILITY AND KINDNESS.

ਸਦਾ ਕੁਰਬਾਨੀ

IS FOREVER SURRENDERING TO YOU

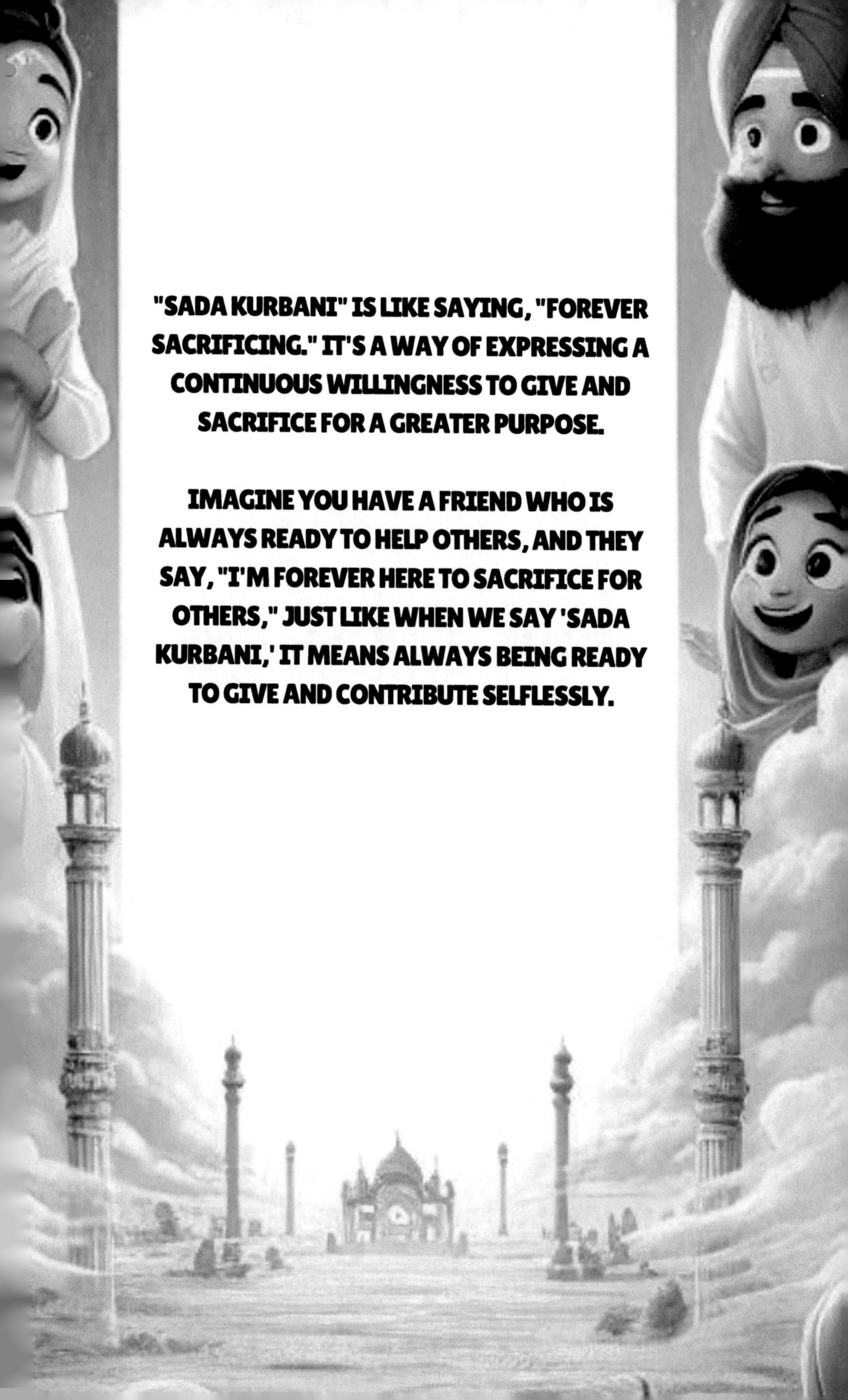

"SADA KURBANI" IS LIKE SAYING, "FOREVER SACRIFICING." IT'S A WAY OF EXPRESSING A CONTINUOUS WILLINGNESS TO GIVE AND SACRIFICE FOR A GREATER PURPOSE.

IMAGINE YOU HAVE A FRIEND WHO IS ALWAYS READY TO HELP OTHERS, AND THEY SAY, "I'M FOREVER HERE TO SACRIFICE FOR OTHERS," JUST LIKE WHEN WE SAY 'SADA KURBANI,' IT MEANS ALWAYS BEING READY TO GIVE AND CONTRIBUTE SELFLESSLY.

Dear Readers,

As I extend my heartfelt gratitude, I am delighted to dedicate this book, "Ardaas: Little Hands, Big Prayers," to my precious daughter, Kyna. Her pure spirit, walking ahead into the Baba Ji room, performing Ardaas for me, fills my heart with immense pride and gratitude.

Kyna, you are a beacon of light, cherishing the profound words of wisdom from our Gurus at such a tender age. Your devotion and love inspire me every day, and it is my deepest wish that this book resonates with your young heart and becomes a source of joy and inspiration.

This labor of love is not just a creation; it's a journey to spread the teachings of our Gurus to young hearts around the world. Each page is infused with the hope that the magic of Ardaas reaches every child, blessing them with the unconditional love of Guru Ji.

I've poured my heart into making this book captivating and inspiring, with the aspiration that it sparks curiosity and warmth in the hearts of young readers. Thank you for joining me on this beautiful journey, and may the blessings of Guru Ji be with each and every one of you.

With love and gratitude,

MS Chadha

Made in the USA
Las Vegas, NV
25 November 2024